A True Book™

Paleontology
The Study of Prehistoric Life

SUSAN H. GRAY

Children's Press®
An Imprint of Scholastic Inc.
New York Toronto London Auckland Sydney
Mexico City New Delhi Hong Kong
Danbury, Connecticut

Content Consultants

Elizabeth Nesbitt, PhD
Curator of Paleontology, Burke Museum
Associate Professor, Earth & Space Sciences Department
University of Washington
Seattle, Washington

Alycia L. Stigall, PhD
Associate Professor, Department of Geological Sciences
OHIO Center for Ecology and Evolutionary Studies
Ohio University
Athens, Ohio

Library of Congress Cataloging-in-Publication Data

Gray, Susan Heinrichs.
  Paleontology the study of Prehistoric life/by Susan H. Gray.
    p. cm.—(A true book)
  Includes bibliographical references and index.
  ISBN-13: 978-0-531-24680-1 (lib. bdg.)   ISBN-10: 0-531-24680-9 (lib. bdg.)
  ISBN-13: 978-0-531-28274-8 (pbk.)   ISBN-10: 0-531-28274-0 (pbk.)
  1. Paleontology—Juvenile literature. I. Title. II. Series.
  QE714.5.G738 2012
  560—dc23   2011030965

All rights reserved. Published in 2012 by Children's Press, an imprint of Scholastic Inc.
Printed in China 62
SCHOLASTIC, CHILDREN'S PRESS, A TRUE BOOK, and associated logos are trademarks and/or registered trademarks of Scholastic Inc.
1 2 3 4 5 6 7 8 9 10 R 21 20 19 18 17 16 15 14 13 12

Find the Truth!

Everything you are about to read is true *except* for one of the sentences on this page.

Which one is **TRUE**?

T or F   The earliest known fossils are about 245 million years old.

T or F   In general, older layers of fossils lie beneath newer layers.

Find the answers in this book.

Contents

THE **BIG** TRUTH!

An ancient shark tooth

Robert Plot ➡
published the first
scientific sketch of
a dinosaur bone.

5

A paleontologist studies dinosaur tracks in almost vertical rock.

CHAPTER 1

The Search for Ancient Life

Have you ever noticed a strange-looking rock at the park or the beach? Maybe it had odd structures in it. It might have contained spirals or stacks of tiny disks. Maybe it seeemed to have a leaf printed on it. Or perhaps the entire rock looked like a bone or a seashell. Rocks such as these are called **fossils**. They contain the remains of ancient living things. Paleontologists study them to learn about life from long ago.

← Fossils are not always found lying flat on the ground.

What a Paleontologist Does

Paleontology is the study of ancient life. Paleontologists use fossils to learn what the earth was like millions or billions of years ago. Fossils are the remains of long-dead plants, animals, and other creatures—their stems, leaves, bones, teeth, shells, and tracks. Paleontologists figure out when the fossilized **organisms** lived. They piece together details of their lives. Paleontologists also study modern-day living things. They compare them to fossilized organisms to see how they are related.

Paleontologists can learn a lot from fossilized eggs.

8

Paleontologists study fossilized nests and even animal droppings.

Paleontologists often travel to faraway places in search of fossils.

Paleontologists are interested in all sorts of things. Some study ancient plants or animals. They might look at tiny organisms as small as one cell! Other paleontologists study fossils to understand what the earth's climate and **ecosystems** were like millions of years ago. These studies help scientists better understand today's climate and how it might change in the future.

Paleontologists travel a lot. Some visit remote places in hot deserts or frozen lands. Some might crawl inside caves that are deep underground.

The early Chinese often believed that powdered fossils could cure illness.

Some stores in China still sell ground-up dinosaur bones as medicine.

CHAPTER 2

The History of Paleontology

Human interest in fossils is hundreds of years old. But people did not always understand what fossils were. Some people believed they rose up inside of rocks. Others thought fossils had dropped from the sky. Still others thought they were just nice things in nature, like flowers. Ancient writers told of "dragon bones" found in China. Experts reading their tales today believe the dragon bones were actually dinosaur fossils.

Steno's New Ideas

Things began to change in the 1660s. That was when the scientist Nicolaus Steno became interested in "tongue stones." For centuries, people had found these mysterious pointed stones. They were embedded in rock located well above sea level. They were called tongue stones because of their shape. Steno compared these stones with the teeth of living sharks. He concluded that tongue stones were actually teeth from long-dead sharks. He proposed that the tooth-bearing rocks had once been under water.

Some ancient shark teeth are much larger than those of modern sharks.

12

Many fossils were found in these cliffs in England in the 1800s.

It is sometimes easy to see where different layers of sediment have formed.

Steno explained that when sea animals died and sank to the seafloor, they were slowly covered with **sediment**. Over time, more animals died, sank, and were covered up. Eventually, many layers of dead animals and sediment formed.

Over millions of years, older sediment layers were pressed into solid rock by the weight and pressure of the younger layers above. As the land changed over time, some of these rocks were pushed above sea level. The rocks dried, crumbled, and cracked. As a result, the fossils within them were exposed.

Steno was ridiculed at first. Many scientists did not agree that fossils were once parts of living organisms. Others accepted Steno's ideas but only in part. Fossilized teeth could be connected to modern animals. But some fossils did not look like anything anyone had seen before.

In 1676, English scientist Robert Plot found a dinosaur thighbone. He concluded it came from a giant human. Other dinosaur finds were said to be the remains of horses, cows, or elephants.

Robert Plot made a careful sketch of the dinosaur thighbone he discovered.

Fossils Become Popular

Before the 1800s, most people did not realize that fossils could be the remains of **extinct** animals. This new concept helped people understand fossils. Many people became interested in them. French scientist Georges Cuvier compared fossil animals to existing animals to better understand ancient animals' lives. Englishman Richard Owen coined the word *dinosaur* to describe three recent discoveries—*Megalosaurus*, *Iguanodon*, and *Hylaeosaurus*. And famed fossil hunter Mary Anning began selling her finds to scientists, schools, and museums.

Mary Anning was called the Princess of Paleontology.

The Bone Wars

By the late 1800s, fossil hunting had reached new heights. In the American West, Edward Drinker Cope and Othniel Charles Marsh competed to discover the most dinosaurs and other extinct creatures. But the race between Cope and Marsh quickly became mean-spirited. Their work was often sloppy and filled with errors. They spied on one another's workers, and even stole from each other's camps. Newspapers called the competition the Bone Wars.

Timeline of Paleontology

1664
Nicolaus Steno develops his ideas on fossils and rock layers.

1676
Robert Plot finds a dinosaur bone and concludes that it is from a giant human.

The Bone Wars led to the discovery of many new dinosaurs, including *Stegosaurus* and *Allosaurus*. The United States became a leader in dinosaur paleontology. But the bitter competition also led to mistakes that took decades to correct. Scientists would have to learn how to cooperate for paleontology to continue to grow.

Today, paleontologists still search for fossils in the field. They also study them in laboratories, under microscopes, and even with special X-rays.

1810–1847
Mary Anning makes many new fossil discoveries.

1842
Richard Owen coins the term *dinosaur.*

A paleontologist takes a look at dinosaur bones found in Alaska.

CHAPTER 3

How Paleontologists See Time

The earth undergoes many changes over time. These changes are preserved in its rock layers. Older layers of sediment and dead organisms are covered by newer layers. These layers eventually turn into sedimentary rock. Paleontologists can compare the contents of one rock layer to those of another. They note differences and similarities between the organisms. This helps them understand how life on the earth changed.

 Scientists once believed that no dinosaurs lived as far north as Alaska.

Slow Changes

Populations of plants and animals change very slowly over generations. As paleontologists discovered more fossils, they began to see how life changed on the earth. When paleontologists look at fossils from **consecutive** layers of sediment, they see changes over time. For example, they have noticed that fossils of land plants are found in more rock layers than the fossils of land animals are.

A paleontologst studies a 600-million-year-old plant fossil in China.

Land plants probably first developed between 500 and 400 million years ago.

Smaller versions of this horsetail fossil still live today.

This means that plants began to spread on land before animals did. Fossils show that the oldest plants were simple and did not have roots. Early plants floated in water. Over time, plants developed root systems that allowed them to hold themselves upright on land. They developed into shrubs, bushes, and trees.

As land plants became more common in the fossil records, more and more plant-eating animals developed. These animals could never have existed before there were enough plants to feed them.

Paleontologists work with geologists to study the earth's past eras.

Dividing Time

Paleontologists have divided the record of life on the earth into three major time spans called **eras**. The earliest is the Paleozoic era, which lasted from about 542 million to 250 million years ago. It was followed by the Mesozoic era, which lasted until about 65 million years ago. The last is the Cenozoic, our current era. Each era is marked by the development—and loss—of certain organisms.

The Paleozoic Era

Simple animals already existed at the beginning of the Paleozoic era. But soon, many new organisms developed. A great variety of worms, corals, clams, snails, fish, insects, amphibians, and reptiles developed. Mosses, ferns, and trees also developed and spread across the land.

Study of the Paleozoic era led scientists to another discovery. Change did not always happen slowly. Sometimes enormous changes happened all at once.

More than 99 percent of species that ever lived on the earth are now extinct.

Diplocaulus was an amphibian that lived at the end of the Paleozoic era.

Trilobites were animals that lived during the Paleozoic era.

Rapid Changes

Around 250 million years ago, huge numbers of **species** became extinct. They are not found in younger rocks. When many plant and animal species become extinct over a short time, scientists call it a mass extinction. Paleontologists use this particular mass extinction to mark the end of the Paleozoic era.

Many factors could play a role in mass extinctions, including volcanic eruptions and changes in climate.

One BIG Discovery

One cold January day in 2003, two college students went fossil hunting. Sarah Kee and Kevin Morgan were digging in an area of Arkansas that they knew was filled with fossils of tiny ocean creatures. Before long, they hit on something big. They called in fellow student Jonathan Gillip to help. The three uncovered the longest *Rayonnoceras*, an ancient relative of the squid, ever found. It was 325 million years old and measured about 8 feet (2.4 meters) long. This was almost three times the length of any other *Rayonnoceras* known.

Sarah Kee (far right), Kevin Morgan, Jonathan Gillip, and their professor

The Facts Behind Mass Extinction

Paleontologists have many questions about why mass extinctions occur. They look for clues in the rock layers. Certain types of rocks and minerals provide information about what was happening when a layer formed. Paleontologists use this information to make guesses about what made species die off.

Volcanoes

Scientists sometimes find layers with a lot of igneous rock. Igneous rocks form when lava cools. A layer with a lot of igneous rock would have formed during a time of great volcanic activity. Too much activity can poison the air and oceans. It can raise the earth's temperature and change weather patterns. Plants could die and plant eaters would starve. With fewer plant eaters around, meat eaters would also starve.

Meteors

Sometimes a layer has large amounts of rare minerals that may have come from meteors. A major meteor impact sends huge amounts of dust into the air. This dust contains certain minerals that are rare on the earth but common in meteors. These minerals settle to the earth and become part of the forming rock layer. Meteor impacts can also create higher temperatures and climate change, leading to mass extinctions.

Life Goes On

Fortunately, the mass extinction at the end of the Paleozoic era did not wipe out everything. Some plants survived. Certain insects, fish, reptiles, and other animals made it through. Paleontologists know this because these organisms' fossils are found in rock that lies above Paleozoic rock. These rock layers mark the beginning of the Mesozoic era. During this time, many new kinds of animals began to develop on the earth.

Paleontologists mark off layers in the rock.

Paleontologists use fossils to figure out how ancient plants and animals looked.

In the Mesozoic era, dinosaurs first developed. Scientists also find the first flower-producing plants and many new species of mammals in the Mesozoic. These changes occurred at the usual slow pace.

But 65 million years ago, there was another mass extinction. Most scientists now understand that it was mostly a result of a meteor impact. Most large land animals, including the dinosaurs, died out in this mass extinction. Sea reptiles and some land plants were also wiped out.

Some ancient species were very small.

One More Time

Just as before, some organisms survived the mass extinction at the end of the Mesozoic era. Dinosaurs were gone for good. But mammals, birds, and other reptiles remained. This new era is called the Cenozoic. Many new mammals and birds developed. Insects **diversified** into the one million species we know today.

Paleontologists agree that there have been at least five mass extinctions during the earth's history. During each one, species across the world were lost. But these massive losses of life have never wiped out everything. And they were always followed by explosive development of brand new species. The species explosion at the end of the Mesozoic era led to the plants and animals we see today.

Some insect fossils consist only of jaws or legs.

Many insect species have existed for more than one million years.

Paleontologists are careful not to cause any damage to the fossils they remove.

CHAPTER 4

The Paleontologists' Tools

Whether they are in the field or in the laboratory, paleontologists use special tools to do their work. In the field, those who hunt for large fossils sometimes use picks and crowbars to pry apart chunks of rock. As they get nearer to the fossils, they must be careful not to damage or break fossils. Therefore, they use smaller tools such as rock hammers, brooms, and paintbrushes to clear rock particles away.

One large rock might contain hundreds of fossils.

From the Field to the Lab

Uncovering fossils that are buried in the earth is challenging work. Bringing them back to the lab can be even more of a challenge. Large fossils in particular require special preparation before they are moved. This is so they do not break before reaching the lab. Field workers cover the fossils in damp tissue paper or aluminum foil. Next, they soak burlap strips in plaster and wrap the fossils. When the plaster dries, it is safe to transport them.

Fossils can be studied more closely after they are transported to museums, laboratories, or universities.

© Julius T. Cs

34

Once the fossils reach the laboratory, workers use pliers and saws to remove them from the plaster. Then they use tiny jackhammers and picks to clean the grit away. Dental tools help clean tiny crevices that are hard to reach. Workers use special glue to stick broken pieces together.

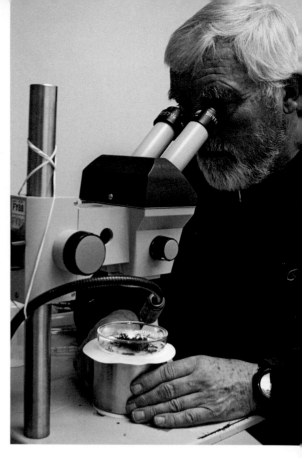

Microscopes are important tools for paleontologists.

To identify the tiniest fossils, paleontologists use powerful scanning electron microscopes. These can show the surfaces of fossilized **pollen** grains and even bacteria. Studying pollen can help scientists learn what kind of plants grew and their role in the ecosystem.

In this photo, the mammoth's tusks stick out of its frozen chunk of earth. The mammoth was kept in a cold ice cave deep underground.

Sometimes, paleontologists are very creative in their tool choices. In 1997, a huge mammoth was discovered in Russia's frozen earth. To get it safely to a lab, scientists first dug around the animal. Next, they had a helicopter transport the chunk of earth that contained the mammoth. After lab workers removed the ice and soil, they used hair dryers to slowly thaw the beast. All of this attention kept the mammoth from falling apart before it was studied.

Delicate Work

Some scientists specialize in preparing fossils for others to study. Fossil **preparators** use miniature instruments to clean fossils. They use little sandblasters and vacuum hoses. Microscopes let them take a closer look at what they are cleaning.

Other workers specialize in rigging up support systems to hold large skeletons in place. This is so the skeleton can be displayed in museums or for study. They use wires, steel rods, screws, and tiny clamps. They do their best to make these supports invisible to viewers.

Once this skeleton is complete, many scientists will be able to study it.

CHAPTER 5

Working Together

Today, paleontologists are involved in many exciting projects. As technology improves, paleontologists are able to learn more and more about fossils and ancient ecosystems. For example, paleontologists once thought that all dinosaurs were covered with scales, plates, or thick hides. However, a closer look at certain fossils tells a different story. Some dinosaurs may have had a coat of primitive feathers.

Some paleontologists have worked as advisers for dinosaur movies.

Colorful Fossils

In some labs, paleontologists are investigating what colors ancient animals were. Fossils generally look dull gray or brown. But new studies have found traces of chemicals and minerals, such as copper, in fossils. They indicate that ancient scales and feathers had certain colors. As these studies continue, we may find out not only what colors some animals were, but how those colors helped these animals survive.

This model presents one guess about how the feathers of the prehistoric Confucius bird were colored.

Coral reefs protect coastlines and provide homes to many different ocean species.

Coral Reefs and Climate Change

Some paleontologists study coral reef fossils. Coral reefs are very sensitive to climate change. Changes in temperature, sea level, and other factors affect their growth. Paleontologists study coral reef fossils to learn about how these organisms reacted to climate change in the past. These studies help scientists better understand how climate change affects coral reefs today and in the future.

Fedexia is named after the shipping service FedEx, which owned the land where the 300-million-year-old reptile skull was found.

New Discoveries

Paleontologists from around the world are discovering new types of mammals, fish, flowers, grasses, and other organisms. The *Sociala* cockroach was a recent find in France. A new relative of the lemur was discovered in western Texas in 2011. The fossil is about 43 million years old!

Understanding these organisms can help us answer questions about the present. It helps us predict the earth's future. But every time a mystery is solved, new questions arise. A paleontologist's work is never done! ★

True Statistics

Age of the earth: About 4.6 billion years

Time of the dinosaurs: From about 230 million to 65 million years ago

Oldest known fossil: A type of bacteria that is thought to be more than 3 billion years old

Largest known flying insect: *Meganeura*, an ancient, giant relative of the dragonfly, with a wingspan of 30 in. (76 cm)

Shortest era: The Cenozoic, only 65 million years so far

Did you find the truth?

 F The earliest known fossils are about 245 million years old.

 T In general, older layers of fossils lie beneath newer layers.

Resources

Books

Bradley, Timothy. *Paleo Bugs: Survival of the Creepiest*. San Francisco: Chronicle Books, 2008.

Farlow, James O. *Bringing Dinosaur Bones to Life: How Do We Know What Dinosaurs Were Like?* New York: Children's Press, 2011.

Hains, Tim. *The Complete Guide to Prehistoric Life*. Ontario, Canada: Firefly Books, 2007.

Holtz, Thomas R. *Dinosaurs: The Most Complete, Up-to-Date Encyclopedia for Dinosaur Lovers of All Ages*. New York: Random House Books for Young Readers, 2007.

Lessem, Don. *The Ultimate Dinopedia: The Most Complete Dinosaur Reference Ever*. Washington, DC: National Geographic Children's Books, 2010.

Peterson, Christine. *Fantastic Fossils*. Edina, MN: Abdo Publishing Company, 2010.

Sloan, Christopher. *Baby Mammoth Mummy Frozen in Time! A Prehistoric Animal's Journey into the 21st Century*. Washington, DC: National Geographic Children's Books, 2011.

Web Sites

**American Museum of Natural History—
PaleontOLogy: The Big Dig**
www.amnh.org/ology/paleontOLogy
Learn about ancient animals, paleontologists, and brand new discoveries at this Web site for kids.

Places to Visit

The Field Museum
1400 South Lake Shore Drive
Chicago, IL 60605-2496
(312) 922-9410
http://fieldmuseum.org
Home of an excellent fossil collection, including Sue, the *Tyrannosaurus rex*.

Museum of the Rockies
600 West Kagy Boulevard
Bozeman, MT 59717
(406) 994-2251
www.museumoftherockies.org
Learn about paleontology through one of the world's biggest collections of dinosaur fossils.

 Visit this Scholastic web site for more information on paleontology:
www.factsfornow.scholastic.com

Important Words

consecutive (kuhn-SEK-yuh-tiv) — one right after the other

diversified (di-VUR-si-fide) — became more varied and different from one another

ecosystems (EE-koh-sis-tuhmz) — communities of living things and the environments they live in

eras (ER-uhz) — long periods of time in history that have some consistent feature

extinct (ik-STINGKT) — no longer found alive

fossils (FAH-suhlz) — preserved bones, shells, footprints, stems, roots, or other traces of ancient life

organisms (OR-guh-nih-zumz) — living things, such as plants or animals

pollen (PAH-luhn) — tiny yellow grains that are the male cells of flowering plants

preparators (pree-PEHR-uh-turz) — people who prepare scientific specimens for study and display

sediment (SED-uh-muhnt) — material such as sand that settles to the bottom of lakes, rivers, and oceans

species (SPEE-sheez) — groups of plants or animals of the same kind and having the same name

Index

Page numbers in **bold** indicate illustrations

About the Author

Susan H. Gray has a master's degree in zoology and has also studied geology and paleontology. She has written more than 120 reference books for children. Susan especially likes to write on topics that engage children in science. She and her husband, Michael, live in Cabot, Arkansas.